The Light as They Found It

The Light

as They

Found It

Poems

James

Seay

William Morrow and Company, Inc.

New York

Grateful acknowledgment is made to the editors of the following publications
in which some of these poems first appeared: *Antaeus:* "Tiffany & Co.";
Carolina Quarterly: "Where Our Voices Broke Off"; *Georgia Review:* "An
Ideal of Itself"; *Gettysburg Review:* "Audubon Drive, Memphis,"
"Cottonmouth, Angus, Redwing," "Not Something in a Magazine"; *New
England Review:* "Night Fires," "When Once Friends"; *New Virginia
Review:* "Cheese"; *Southern Humanities Review:* "Faith as an Arm of
Culture, Culture as an Arm of Narration," *"The Weather Wizard's Cloud
Book."* The poems "Clouds over Islands" (in a slightly different version) and
"Where Our Voices Broke Off" appeared in a limited edition by Deerfield
Press/Gallery Press (Ireland) and were reprinted in *The Made Thing: An
Anthology of Contemporary Southern Poetry.* "Mountains by Moonlight" was
commissioned by the Mint Museum, Charlotte, North Carolina, and is in
response to collages by T. S. Sullivan.

The author would like to thank the North Carolina Arts Council and the
National Endowment for the Arts for a jointly supported grant that helped
him complete this book.

Library of Congress Cataloging-in-Publication Data

Seay, James L.
The light as they found it : poems / James Seay.
p. cm.
ISBN 0–688–08932–1 / 0–688–10020–1 (pbk)
I. Title
PS3569.E24L53   1990
811'.54—dc20   90–8301
                                        CIP

Printed in the United States of America

First Edition

1 2 3 4 5 6 7 8 9 10

BOOK DESIGN BY CYNTHIA KRUPAT

for my mother,

Lucie Belle Page Seay,

and my sisters,

Jackie and Donna,

ladies all

Contents

I

When Once Friends

I can tell this fairly quick,
the two narrative lines sharing a common angle
and there being mist in both instances.
As for why my friend and I
were running a rented fishing boat
through morning fog on dead reckoning,
it was a matter of wanting to arrive early and alone
at the shrimp farm where sea trout
were working along the fence for strays.
More than anything I remember the angle,
something sure and strict in my reading,
of the cabin cruiser that came out of the fog
and crossed our bow close enough for us
to know again it was not our special selves
or anything our wives knew about greyhounds
that had paid us eleven-to-one on two-dollar bets
at the dog track the night before.
A name on the racing form more lyric than the next,
a combination of favored colors in the silks,
the worn luck of the draw,
was what bought us beer in green bottles
instead of cans for the weekend.
The cruiser never looked back
at my friend and me and our luck
rolling in their wake.
The other angle was of a plane in the clouds,

_____

the only time I've ever been ferried by private charter.
Going up through cloud cover
the young pilot said he didn't have radar
and had never been to where I was going,
so we'd have to come back down through the clouds
in a calculated while and look around for a landmark.
His co-pilot pointed to a symbol
for a checkered water tower on the chart.
All I could add to the basic rhopalic of clock,
compass, and radio was another eye,
the one pointing my finger toward the Cessna
that had just slipped through the gauze
of our future like a cruiser
and laid down for the second time in my life
the providential angle.
Those twin incidents were long
ago and whatever has made
my friend remote and finally silent
as he goes about his days
is as hidden to me as the way two such moments
could conform so in texture and geometric circumstance.
One other thing:
after we found the water tower
and were parked on the runway,
the pilot walked around the nose of the plane
to where I was standing with my bags.

———

He reached up and broke a sleeve of ice
from the leading edge of the wing
and offered half to me.
His co-pilot had forgotten to fill the water jug.
After a few minutes of small talk
he taxied up the runway
lifting into the overcast winter.
I stood there beside the one road leading in,
waiting for my ride and thinking of how the morning
cleared on the wide sound
and we caught the speckled trout
our wives broiled with pimiento and Parmesan,
lemon and parsley.
We drank the beer in green bottles,
saying the wonderful names of the winning hounds
all through the evening.
That was what I remembered that winter day
and what I remember now is both that and the angle—
and standing there on the small runway,
eating the ice of unknowing alone,
its cloud, where we had been.

Tiffany & Co.

Leafing through a friend's catalogue—
the Fall Selections 1987—
I linger on something the blue of a robin's egg
and wonder why I've never bought any of these *objets*,
never felt the specific fetish-force
of the commodity behind the revolution
of their brass doors or 800 number.
There's possibly history to explain:
we could go back, say, seventy years
to when my mother and JFK were born
and take a look around:
Freud's new Intro to Psychoanalysis on one hand,
Lenin entering the Winter Palace on the other,
but mainly there's the paradigmatic news
every winter day in Tyro, Mississippi,
of no indoor plumbing and a dead aunt's
five children extra to feed,
which lasted right on through my kindergarten
of visits to Granny's.
                    So why on Bolshaya Morskaya
would I go looking for Fabergé's old St. Petersburg shop
when where Lenin had breakfast
with smoldering Bolsheviks was just around the corner?
Well, maybe to have pissed into both the figurative
wind and a hole in the ground
is to be drawn to the abstract gloss

---

of privilege as though it might incorporate
and invite us to its private Mardi Gras—
such parades in life, for instance, as lunch
with the woman in Georgetown
whose every emblem was Camelot,
right down to sterling frame for the Presidential scrawl
on a scrap of teletype
thanking her for the intro to Ian Fleming
and 007.
But it didn't seem, on Bolshaya Morskaya, the same dream
of Fat Tuesday's carnival and masquerade.
I thought of old Fabergé, Russian to the bone and in Swiss exile
while Bolsheviks, quit with eating fable-cake,
were already breaking rank and bellying up
to the tsar's bar, the monkey
of power settling on their backs,
jeweled eggs glittering in their words.
Power's not like Bond's regimental gin;
it wants to be stirred never shaken:
sooner or later there's the commissioned aria,
the room of shoes worn once or never,
cinema's kitten purr.
Or the threadbare velvet glove
on the stainless steel hand
the cautious in any century recognize.
                              She didn't smile—

my Intourist guide in Moscow—
but I meant it only as a joke
when I asked her if there was a tunnel
between the headquarters of the KGB
and the country's largest store of children's toys,
just across the street.
One imperial egg in the Kremlin nearby
still has as its surprise the miniature
Trans-Siberian Railway train.
Another opens to reveal Nicholas's yacht
scaled down in gold.
We have to imagine the crossties & rails, the constant steppes,
in all seasons, to the sea,
imagine the sea as well, and the globe
we want to shape and shape again.

Faith as an Arm of Culture,

Culture as an Arm of Narration

All those miles, the dark water beneath us
as we slept in the wide rows.
From Heathrow, jet-lagging and hugging the left
eight hours into the moors
to walk through the open gate
beside the flower garden and find it—
right where she said on the transatlantic telephone,
my friend Bonnie from Georgia,
away for the weekend with her fiancé in France:
the back door key
up under the mop bucket,
her grandmother's language and habit.

Time Open-Faced Yet Secret Before Us

(for Roy, who thought he wrote the book on bricks)

I
One of the last places you'd look,
but it's there
on the floor between the wall and my stove:
a small digital clock
blinking hours and minutes
I'd probably fish out with gum or tape
if it weren't for the notion of time fallen
by chance beyond the senses almost and secret.

II

Even with watches
we lost all track of time
the time we drank all the high proof
rum we could find
and pour plain on ice in the clear jumbo plastic
cups the woman at the package store
in Crawfordville gave us when we crawled out
of the Wakulla wet and wild with our best
anecdote of the week.
All my buddies could shout about
was how the light and speed,
not to mention focus,
better have been right or I had
had it as captain even of my own craft.
I'd set the time-release
and slipped into the water with them
to look laughing into the lens
while the camera floated from us
on the bow of the boat.
At the very moment the shutter tricked
time for our yearly group portrait
dog-paddling in the middle of the river,
somebody looked around and found the alligator
surfaced among us, a confluence of events like no
other we could remember later that night

———

at the roadhouse restaurant eating fried shark
and beating on the table with the hilarity
of danger we were already hyping up for history.
And not a one of us could have told
the time, whether it was space
measured by time-honored points on our boat:
the bow being noon
where the alligator rose to our surprise,
or whether it was what we hoped had been
inscribed knot-eyed and ancient among us,
still secret in the chemical film,
or what the waitress,
weary with hearing our four-hour punch line,
weary with Hwy 98 driving the same
story all day and night
into Panacea Florida's penultimate
worst restaurant, said it was:
time to put the chairs on the tables, boys.
Of all my father has lost
since the war,
he told me he missed most
his photographs from overseas.
I think of his old Argus camera
hauled from island to island
in the pack with K rations and extra rifle clips,
as though each were needed

to validate the other.
Only the most disingenuous among us would deny
we want the light and speed
to be right
so that we shine in our fathers' eyes.
I don't know what else held us so
to the anecdote of danger,
but there was something outside the narrative
line, outside the hope of future proof
we had been there,
outside even the desired focus
of attention from another—
something close to living both
in the moment and in the option.

———

III

Not much was left
except the floor beams
and stone foundation by the time
we topped the hill on foot
two centuries later.
That, and a view time hadn't much touched.
She may never have forgotten
what she knew of England—
may have returned there
or gone elsewhere eventually—
but if the way she scanned
the Blue Mountains
in the green Jamaican distance daily
didn't come to be a permanent measure
in her dreams
I don't understand what's a lovely haze
of ridges and foliage rising
and falling in this world.
I'm thinking of the plantation owner's daughter.
She had first to get over the loss
of her mother, taken by fever soon after arriving,
and besides sickness there was unrest.
Even the favored house servants
stole away into the mountains
with the field slaves one night.

———

I am thinking, though, of their times—
father, daughter, fugitive
slaves, neighbors on the faraway roads—
along with us
outside the currencies of sugar and bananas
and fresh boatloads of blacks from Angola, Ghana,
wherever the world's sweet tooth bites sharpest.
I am thinking of how
at times the daughter
would go to the basement
and gaze into the brilliant day
or crescent moon through gun slits
her father had fashioned in the stone foundation
when it was laid.
I don't want her to sound
too exotic or romantically wistful.
While she had both the dreamy inclination
and an edge made keen by fine feeling,
she was capable of taunting
at least the younger blacks
and she more than once came close
to torturing cats in the cistern shed.
By the time we got there
it was all goats and ganja.
This was well off
what the travel brochures call

the beaten track,
and we wouldn't have been there
if my friend hadn't had a friend
who had needed an alternative
to his life in the States
and bought this goat farm
we could now visit.
He and his girlfriend gave us to understand
they sold only goats to the natives.
I remember their faces, sweet enough,
but not their names.
What lodges in memory is the daughter
and father's fallen-down house
we stumbled on,
the floorless mahogany beams above me
I wanted for my own,
and the gun slits in the stone foundation—
narrow vertical frames
beveled on the basement's interior side,
I remember, rather than on the outside
facing the surrounding mountains,
a slight architectural detail so pure
and simple that something of their lives
was given to me in a way
no page or moving picture could
without the very light around me—

———

something like an option
outside the lethal fact
of a bevel cut on the interior surface
of a wall to allow the widest angles
for their guns
yet not funnel, as an exterior bevel
would, what they had made
of race and station back
into their faces in the breach.
In my mind, his mind
and hand free almost of the imperial moment
and impulse, the chalk mark
on the stone for cutting, his letter
gone out across the North Atlantic
that they could book passage
to come in the spring.
But lodged more strongly
than any beveling for simple survival
is the message she left
in the enigma of metaphor
scratched years later beside one
of those same openings into the blue
In your chimney of love,
count me ten brick.
Tell me the measure, timekeepers:
stinting or taking the long view

---

that knows we are given so
widely to this world
that ten would be plenty
from any single hand pledging
to help hold warmth and focus what's not
needed into the blue.
But what do I know
of love or loss turned
to such a figure?
I can imagine her only so far.
It could have been a local
joke or private saying;
it could have been
ten clandestine days and nights inside
what passed for love
or an announcement of minimal intent.
The chimney was gone
and our goat-farmer/ganja-man
knew of the house solely by rumor.
The view from the opening
she chose to leave her words beside
is the same as from the tall south windows
I imagine above,
but she is down here—
and not because there is danger.
For now, the smoke plumes of slaves

escaped to the mountains are domestic
in nature, and vague, simply part of the view.
I don't have anyone in mind for her.
There are these words
she wants someone to find—father
or lover?—and there is the optional
way in her mind space and time
are bordered and measured here.
Even with the roof and floor
vanished I see how
the dazzle of light is doubled in the small slit,
her time of love fallen by chance
before me almost, yet secret.
She is gazing toward the rise and fall
of ridge-line and clouds drifting inland
from the Caribbean,
her hand on the beveled stone
foreign and tentative
but alive with this
other way of being.

Clouds over Islands

First there was a dream not wholly mine.

I told my friends the dream
comes with the bed, its source a cloud
accumulated in the air surrounding sleep.

Just off the plane, I had dozed on their bed
as they swam in the screened pool, promising
I would like the crabs at Joe's Stone Crabs,
the daughter would be off the phone in my room
shortly, she was in love. The migrant dream
settled around me as the rhythm of the laps they swam
defined the rhythm of my breathing.

When I woke it took their voices
from beside the pool for me to know
I had breathed the dream
from the cloud above their private island of sleep.

The dream itself does not matter
in its particulars,
not even to my friends.
Nor could I have told it clearly, its cloud
so tropic and brief in my life.

I told them of a family I knew in Ohio
who bought the childhood furniture

———

of a famous astronaut, his little bed and mattress,
the strange vast air
in which the family's daughter began to dream.

Then together we remembered confusions
in the expired air over beds we had held
in hotels, hospitals, the compartments of trains,
or rooms of senility where our grandfathers called back
the gifts they had given us,
how sometimes still we rise from sleep in beds
where no friends have breathed dreams
we can enter without fear,
how we stumble to our belongings,
trying to make sure of what we left there.

Where Our Voices Broke Off

From the porch, if they hold to what there is
no need to imagine, they can color the hedge,
the sound, the lighthouse with its pattern of black
and white lozenges, or the air over the island
and anything lofted in its translations.
My sons turn their brushes instead to the chronic
bad dreams of the race, fixing them at random
in the watercolors of flame or collision.
They are old hands at apostrophe.
The shrimper's son from across the road tries a few circles
and then begins the outline of a boat.

Last night from this porch I looked up
with my wife and friends to our share
of the galaxy, whorled pure and free of mainland lights.
I felt our voices drawn out into the dark
and it seemed to me the round island was a stone
turning beneath us, grinding our voices with the shells
of shrimp in the kitchen pail, the quilts by the door,
the hyphens in the names of boats at anchor—all of it drawn
and turning under the stone—the drums of paint
for the lighthouse diamonds, the bright water that breaks
on shoals and jetties, whatever yields to silence, ground
with our voices and spread like grist across the spaces.

One of the Dippers brought us out of silence
and we began working our way through the known.

For the constellations we could not name
we imagined *Cricket's Knee, Bill & Doris' Blown Electric Range,*
Anne's New Rod & Reel, Tommy's Measles, and so on
until we all were found.
We called it The Myth of the New Understanding.
It was a way of turning from the silence beyond the porch
railing, the silence in the hedge along the road
and out across the sound to the lighthouse.
It was a way of understanding the lights
burning their codes through darkness.

The boat is colored yellow and the water blue.
It is headed to the left of the paper,
under what appears clear weather.
Toward dawn we saw his father make fast the mooring
and load his catch into a skiff.
I do not know if he looks up at the stars at sea
and wonders what is at the farthest reach of darkness
or if he dwells on whether the shrimp are vanishing.
I do not know if he has told his son of the silent migrations.
He declined the beer.
We bought the shrimp still moiling in the bucket.

23

What Words For

Bougainvillea, hibiscus, weeping fig?—
the Cuban let us walk along and point instead.
Leaving we looked like a rolling greenhouse.
There are larger terms for life and death, I know,
but wedged in the rearview mirror
among coolers of fish for the freezer,
Ficus benjamina was the one I fixed my hopes on.
Ficus, fig, whatever you want to call it,
the idea was it would somehow lift
the ailing one at home, its own genderless kind,
or, failing that, replace it in the cachepot
centering the living room window.
So we were something tropical
and self-commissioned coming north on I-95.
Part of the shading of tone, though, was how
our one-armed fishing guide had outdone us both.
But even with that nuance, ambient and humbling,
all the way from the Keys, it never dropped a leaf.

In all of this, the notion somehow our lives
are linked to them for more than the mere air.
There are reasons the Haitians
painted their small, almost toy, boat in bright stripes
of green and red and other reasons
they sailed it to where we had found it
confiscated and beached near Islamorada.

             The ailing one at home,
for instance, I would falter
if it followed through on what sometimes seems
a drift toward barrenness or surrender.
For the move from Nashville thirteen years ago
I wrapped it in wet sheets
and then wrapped that in clear plastic.
I asked the mover if he would load it last,
in the rear of the van, and open the doors
halfway through June and the interstate to Carolina
for a little sun.

What I mean too is how they seem at times
to turn from us, a kind of judgment
they have no words for, only this dropping
of leaves, or that paling, from what has passed
through the room where it is not in the light
to be constant, how even now
the ficus that was green and flourishing
from the Cuban's smile, part of our cargo
of acceptable compromise and materiality—Igloos full
of cobia and dorado and redfish we would share,
the capital of a column I salvaged
from old resort architecture dumped against erosion,
a tarred hat with a Rebel Lures logo Made in Korea
we found in the tide—how even now

———

that one I saw something of the green future in
is turning and nearly sere.
Ah little sister, little brother,
children everywhere.

Inside, Outside,

the Dialectics Once More

How could we have known or cared with our tourist cameras
whether it was Sterno or Campbell's Soup?
The hook was how he had disconnected
the lights on the Christmas tree
outside the Church of the Heavenly Rest
and plugged his hot plate into the only extension cord
he could find in the east Eighties.
That, and maybe the fact our heads were full of van Gogh.
The cipher, that is, of the same hand holding and letting go:

we had wondered for hours at the nearly ninety canvases
of the final year and a summer,
seventy of them done in as many days, the numbers alone
a closure we couldn't shake off.
Like the others in the museum line
we looked for signs of ultimate intent,
the *suppressio veri* he had surely coded for detection
so that we would overtake him on the road outside Auvers
before he reached the suicide field.

But except for crows over a wheat field
we were left with olive trees and cypresses,
the great starry night, irises, two views of Daubigny's garden.
If most of that seems to spiral from cyclotrons
or strain toward fission like a vision of nuclear day,
consider its valency also in the way of life

coming back around to life in the constant cosmic charities.
So what was our evidence finally
but a further calculus of alternatives?

Another portrait of how we might be lifted and turned
was the Oriental woman high in the bell tower
on Christmas Day. I raised my camera once,
then let it drop unshuttered, the way her eyes were shut
and taking in the sun glancing off the river,
the way her hands rested
on the railing around the carillonneur's booth
as French and Dutch carols pealed from the tons of bells
and shook even the stones that held us there.

If the portrait seems a Zen cliché almost,
consider that I mean also the way Rockefeller millions
had put Handel finally in the air around us
nearly four hundred feet over Riverside, the way her coat
was crimson against her black hair, her butterfly bow
whimsical and silver in the winter light.
Consider that later as my son and I ate the sushi & sashimi
combination on Christmas afternoon, something
we had planned days before, we talked as much of the double-

square canvases van Gogh had turned to at the very end
or of photographs we might have had

———

as of anything Eastern or otherworldly.
One final turn, though: if our talk seems remote
from the events and unrelated to the chemistry of warm sake
or how as we walked out onto Broadway near sunset
the light was the light of boulevards and fields held
in the pledge of return, consider that we knew containment was not
those formal things alone, the way the world everywhere we found it

seemed something other than other.

II

Audubon Drive, Memphis

There's a black and white photo of Elvis
and his father Vernon in their first swimming pool.
Elvis is about twenty-one and "Heartbreak Hotel"
has just sold a million.
When he bought the house,
mainly for his mother Gladys they say,
it didn't have a pool,
so this is new.
The water is up to the legs of Vernon's trunks
and rising slowly as he stands there
at attention almost.
Elvis is sitting or kneeling on the bottom,
water nearly to his shoulders,
his face as blank and white
as the five feet of empty poolside at his back.
The two of them are looking at the other side
of the pool and waiting for it to fill.
In the book somewhere
it says the water pump is broken.
The garden hose a cousin found is not in the frame,
but that's where the water is coming from.
In the background over Vernon's head you can see
about three stalks of corn
against white pickets in a small garden
I guess Gladys planted.
You could press a point and say that in the corn

and the fence, the invisible country
cousin and mother, the looks on Elvis's and Vernon's
faces, the partly filled pool, we can read
their lives together, the land
they came from, the homage they first thought
they owed the wealth beginning to accumulate,
the corny songs and films,
and that would be close but not quite central.
Closer than that is the lack
of anything waiting in the pool we'd be
prompted to call legend
if we didn't know otherwise.
They're simply son and father wondering if it's true
they don't have to drive a truck
tomorrow for a living.
But that's not it either.
What it reduces to is the fact that most of us
know more or less everything
that is happening to them
as though it were a critical text
embracing even us and our half-mawkish
geographies of two or three word obituaries:
in the case of Kennedy, for example, I was walking
across a quad in Oxford,
Mississippi; King's death too caught me in motion,
drifting through dogwood in the Shenandoah.

———

As for Elvis,
there were some of us parked outside a gas station
just over the bridge from Pawley's Island
with the radio on.
That's enough.
I know the differences.
But don't think they're outright.
The photo is 1034 Audubon Drive, Memphis,
and then it's Hollywood,
still waiting for the pool to fill.

Not Something in a Magazine

It was intelligent enough, what the photographer had been saying
as I drifted out the door. Something about Susanne Langer on
    metaphor.
That there was as much for me in the moon and stars
tilting in the oval mirror I held at angles to the summer sky
is a measure of nights and days with so little glamour
I'd just as soon forget how I tried first to find my face
in the mirror mounted on the stranger's dresser,
left for some reason overnight in the yard across from the party
    I'd abandoned.
Yard sale, fresh paint, bad memories, I don't know why.
What I remember, after the cliché of self seen in shadow and
    silhouette,
is turning the mirror on its hinges heavenward
and standing there shifting from one oval of night to another.
Readings have come to take the place of genuine witness,
she said in her book, referring to the reflectors and signals of
    science
and how the finality of sense-data was the cue of a former epoch.
The week before I'd watched the clerk at the hardware store
hammer out my name a letter at a time on a brass tag for my dog
and as he neared the end I realized I was following his hand
letter by letter with the notion that he was pulling from an alphabet
that would spell me in a different way to the dream I had of myself.
But the final die, Y, came from between the X and Z I'd always
    known.

———

I didn't mean by *glamour* something in a magazine.
At its roots it draws on knowing and mystery circling within desire
like a system almost, but constant only in its moment,
a grammar of signs transformed and transforming.
I know the dreamer over the pool was not a genuine witness
or scientist of the first water, reading himself alone in the mediate
    thing.
And I know you weren't out there, pilgrim, with the mirror
horizontal in your hands, panning the oval waters like a fool,
but you understand: maybe something renewable in the skittering
    light,
maybe a likeness we could carry back across the street and call our
    own.

Cheese

1.

One thing touches on another.

2.

My youngest uncle usually smelled like cheese
until he discovered women.
The eyes and ears of the world
were all on war, but he was classified 4-F
owing to a broken back in his medical records
and couldn't go.
So he found himself among more women
than he could ever get around to
at the cheese plant where they all worked
for the war effort.
Before the women, he brought it home in loaves,
snugged under his jacket sleeves like dive bombs.
He told me how it was made
and how they weren't allowed
to eat any on the job.
We sat at night and ate the war cheese with saltines
until he started going out
with the women and wearing colognes.

3.

Years later I was processing a compensation claim
for an insurance company I was working for.
A rural woman was claiming the cheese
at the plant where she worked
had infected her finger.
She said she had suffered with it long enough
and wanted money for her pain.
I recorded her testimony at the farm
where she lived alone with her mother,
but I was thinking the whole time of my uncle
and how different it had been at his cheese plant.
When I played back the tape later in the car
I could hear roosters in the background—
crowing for their cheese, I guess.

4.

The other night at a college party
some students told me that eating cheese
is when you eat a woman.
I looked around at all the cheese in the room
and I thought of my uncle's wan smile:
more cheese than he ever dreamed
yet he wanted to be overseas.
I thought of the grown woman living at home
with her swollen finger, dreaming of money
for her pain from cheese.
I thought of the daughters in party linen,
pastels and fragrances so varied and fragile I'd never have
thought cheese on my own
or how it had to do with anything they wanted of life.
But there they were,
full and ripe as their mothers,
edible in the given figure,
though unaware of the overlap that brought them
into that moony congress in my mind, all of us duped
by this or that, our faces nonetheless
brightening with the word on our lips *cheese*
for any likeness, any touch of the future—
cheese, for whatever it means.

Easter Sunrise,

the Constant Moon We Settled For

All we knew was look low to the southeast,
but that was where the waning gibbous moon
and the one mercury vapor light on the island
had more or less taken over the horizon.
So we moved to another dune that at least
put the mercury vapor behind an eave
of the beach house being built next door.
The Atlantic hummed so steady in a strip of loose aluminum
in the half-done duct system that my son
joked how probably it was the workers still there.
They'd been drinking beer
all day Saturday and mixing country & western
with things like Jerry Lee Lewis
and Sting's new blue turtle album.
It isn't hard to figure how they'd believe most of that
more than the story of a carpenter
orbiting life and death
forever or how it would seem pointless
to make a sunrise service even of this comet
my son and I and our friend were trying to substantiate.
Finally we had to turn the telescope to the moon.
I don't know to this day if the only candidate
I could find for the comet was Deneb in Cygnus
or the tensed star in Sagittarius's shoulder
or simply Venus in the morning shuttle.
Or one of the others I read in a text.

———

Whichever, we couldn't hang enough of a tail on it
to offer as the once in a lifetime gift
we'd promised our ladies drowsing on sofas inside.
We settled instead for the great Sea of Rains,
Mare Imbrium, one of the moon-man's eyes.
We settled for Tycho and its system of rays,
worn in another story as the Lady's amulet.
We settled for the Rabbit's head, our Ocean of Storms.
That was the story of things until dawn.
There were usually new shoes for me and my sisters on Easter.
Part of the myth was how my grandmother
used to shine my mother's black patents with a biscuit.
The man beyond the bridge to Swansboro that afternoon
came out of his trailer with a beer still in his hand
when his dog wouldn't stop barking.
We'd seen the FOR SALE sign
from the car and thought how desuetude
such as that inside and out of the house moldering
next to a trailer couldn't bring much more than twenty thousand
or so and we could maybe get a second mortgage
to fix it up for a tumbledown vacation lodge.
But the man said the deal included the nearmost lot
and rented trailer he'd been living in since the Air Force.
I saw he didn't want to have to leave the view:
when we asked if he knew the owner's price
he pointed to the Intracoastal

Waterway and the shuttle
of bright boats beyond his screened porch.
The way he said three hundred and fifteen thousand
told me it was all to him like light-years I can't understand
either or quite believe in, how one light
that reaches my eye was breaking from stone
the morning my mother's mother
was taking a biscuit from the oven
and another light tonight maybe having started out even
before Earth's sun was born.
Standing there beside the sign
I could count in my mind the channel markers
leading back up the Intracoastal to the inlet
that swept past our rented cottage on the island.
I could hear the strip of loose aluminum
over the distance that had hummed the whole weekend
to remind me somebody had the hard cash or easy credit
for this world. Listen, I had dreamed that last remaining lot
on the Point as mine more than once.
But I don't know what it would have taken to own the end
of an island any more than I know
where we thought we'd get twenty thousand
for Easter afternoon on the mainland.
I was thinking of the water and the light.
I've bought up whole coastlines that way, whole mountains.
So there we were—stargazers, comet seekers, workers boozed

and clocking overtime for strangers we never saw,
frontage owners, veterans in doublewides
with dogs hooked to clotheslines for news
they don't want to hear, one magnitude
after another of debt and credit and doubt—
and I thought of how sometimes it has to be enough
to settle for the moon, any music that matches the ellipse
of our lives.
I thought of how sometimes we have
to settle for whatever view there is,
though what we believe is the water running clean
with the tide of light reappearing morning after morning.

The Weather Wizard's Cloud Book

(to LDR, Jr.)

Of the clouds your father
photographed, you must remember most
those that day in the drizzle
as you stepped down from the trolley
and found him with his camera cloaked
and angled toward that part of the firmament
he needed to fix and leave with us,
his own record of weather's quirky provenance.

And how the weather of your youth
must have turned suddenly gray and sodden
within you, this man your father,
hunched over in the middle of the street,
photographing the worthless sky—or the rain
itself for all she knew, the girl you'd brought home
to meet the family, to somehow impress,
there, O lost, on your arm, a rigid adolescent silence.

Last month I touched a stone
that Thomas Wolfe's father had worked
into a doorstop for his bride-to-be.
J.E.W. FROM W.O.W. 1884
was all it said, and we can read
into that the coming remoteness that drove them
to Dixieland, by which I mean her literally
to her boardinghouse and Tom to the found door

of fiction. By which I mean too
you couldn't have known, there on the street
with your miserable teenage angst,
in what ways clouds were his meaning, likenesses struck
in black and white and Kodachrome for his book.
Nor could you have known your turning away was old hat
as sons go—sky, wet leaves and tarmac, red scarf all a book,
one book always a door to another, our story of loss never lost.

Johnny B. Goode

You couldn't count the times
Chuck Berry has duck-walked that song across the stage.
I'd say the draw is mostly rock and roll,
though I could probably write one of those pop-culture essays
on its all-American iconography,
the railroad running through the promise-land
and Johnny strumming to the rhythm the drivers made,
not to mention lost Eden
way back up in the woods among the evergreens.
We might hear all of that at some level,
I guess, and there must be a kind of dramatic imperative
in his name we have to cheer for beyond rock and roll.
It's left tentative whether Johnny will see himself
in lights, but we know he's more than nominally good
and'll honor every tender dream his mother ever had.
It doesn't matter that the paradise of lights
is like any other paradise, a paradox down to its roots,
a walled-in park we die to get out of,
and that finally Johnny is going to be singing those songs
about wanting country roads to take him home,
back in time to the evergreens.
It doesn't matter because Johnny has got to get
into the Coupe de Ville just like Maybelline did,
the promise in every song they've ever heard.
And when we pull alongside in the V-8 Ford
we're barely going to be able to tell them apart

———

through the tinted glass: the one we're cheering for
and the one we're asking why can't she be true.

Cottonmouth, Angus, Redwing

I was the one afloat on a film
of metal, nearly motionless in the pond
and thinking mine was the only language
in the riddle of three creatures
that had come to the water in unison.
I know that even with the paddle and fly-rod
stock-still I was an array of heat and sound
signals across the water—and a reckoned symbol
constant in the eye of the cottonmouth
that slipped from a copse of willows
and swam to the facing shore in an unbroken succession of S's,
but the seeming heedlessness,
the no-need-to-talk-to-me, the fix of direction,
put me to thinking of the phylum
and our possible distinction—man, the thinking animal—
as though I were a sophomore again.
If the lowing of the Aberdeen Angus bull
brought the rest of the clan down the hill,
what was that syntax finally but an ecclesiastic set
of testicles so pendulous they swayed like something rung?
Not even the red-winged blackbird would signal anything more
than the silent semaphore of sex,
a quick dark blur coming at me and then its flash of red,
its veering spaceward.
I've since read that they know more than we think,
how a cat's spitting hiss, for instance,

is maybe mimicry playing on the world's fear of snakes.
So we could say the sorting out in the reptilian center,
the bellowing, the vaunted sexual plumage,
and what the Audubon Guide calls
a "gurgling, liquid *conk-kar-ree*, running up the scale
and ending in a trill,"
is all a kind of red-winged cotton-mouthed Angus language.
I think of how it veered and was gone,
and now I see myself alone—
the one differently verbed,
the one with time on my hands,
stopping to wonder, to remember a woman loved
and lost because we were not what we said.
Then I began again to put barbs
flying in the air,
none of them a part of my body.

Mountains by Moonlight

The postcard artist Harry Martin
could have gone to Mars
and not found a better full moon
for his Mountains by Moonlight.
It looks like a photograph
that's been hand-tinted and stars added.
When they were young
our grandparents sent it home
wishing everyone was there in the space
for writing messages.
The matte finish softens the moonlight
to where it's almost melancholy.
We don't know whether to lie down
and embrace our aloneness together on earth
or fly to the moon.
It's pure nature,
not a Model T or AAA sign in sight,
but we know that outside the frame
the technology's in place for flight,
organ transplants, just about anything
you could imagine.
We know that beyond the mountains by moonlight
there is an architecture
our grandparents had to leave finally
in the same way they left these mountains.
We know that when we draw arrows,

as they did, to hotel windows
it's both to separate ourselves
from the sheer sameness of things *my room*
was here and yet double the evidence
we were part of that sameness
my room was there.
Once for a magazine article
I located Scott Fitzgerald's room
at the Grove Park Inn in Asheville
by standing in the parking lot
and counting up to the window
he had x'd on a postcard.
From the terrace he could see
the lights of Highland Hospital
where Zelda thought she was talking
to Christ and William the Conqueror and Mary Stuart.
Not even the mountains by moonlight
could put him to sleep,
so he took Luminal and Amytal
and a young married woman from Memphis.
Two years later he was in Hollywood.
We don't know if it was silliness
or loneliness that prompted the postcard
he sent to himself at the Garden of Allah
where he had rooms.
When they came home they brought us honey

———

in small jars shaped like bears,
assembly-line tom-toms with rubber heads,
cities we could shake into blizzards.
They asked if we got the cards.
Next year it would be palm trees
and a crescent moon.
We couldn't imagine them under those moons
with anything other than hearts
lifting to the broadened horizon.
We couldn't imagine them as having ever doubted
the light as they found it.

Night Fires

(for Beth)

I
If it's true that we don't know
our own hearts, or that we're rarely talking
about what we think we're talking about,
or that there're always at least two others
under the covers with us,
then we might just as well believe
that each of the simple moments we've tried
to hold for our lives
is its complex opposite, or close.
In which case the lamp's new mantle
in its first converting blaze from silk
to ash filament carried instead of our wonder
the final neural failure of bluefish
on ice in the Igloo cooler,
and we ate those fish in lemon and sweet butter
with a mind to the world's loss.
Likewise we should try to forget
the tiny lights
of Emerald Isle and Salter Path
blinking dreamily across the inlet and playing
in the mesh window of our tent.
No, each of those motions took hold
of time on a simple plane,
gathering with them the clean curves of our small boat
Spoondrift, anchored long-line and lifting

high-bowed in the blue-green tide,
the bunted clouds, the elderly kite collector's
mylar and nylon and rice paper
from all over the world, the dragons and streamers
he looped the whole weekend like carnivals.
Our tent was a comic feather
in the sea wind
until we staked it deeper,
laughing and stumbling in the dark.
And then we zipped ourselves in,
high on that dune with our little window to the water.

II

But I'm thinking too about how children want
to be over the deepest part.
As the house gets louder with bourbon
and basting the holiday venison at midnight
they skate alone with a cousin
on the pond that was slush at noon,
pressing closer to the center with each sweep.
It's that moment I have in mind,
neared by simple arcs,
but without the fatal prospect,
if that's possible.
I think of the night
on the North Yorkshire moor far from town
when we came upon the glowing
that looked first like a cavern
within which the deepening earth was on fire.
The next morning we found the great fallen tree
whose center even still was a far chamber
of embers for no reason we could understand.
If it had been a lake the night before
that did not burn us
we would have skated farther and farther out.

———

IV

Gifts Divided

This morning the light lay across the table
in a way that lifted
from the shallow of a favored bowl the tincture
of petals I floated there

half without a plan over the course of a year
I had hoped long lost.
A simple fingerbreadth of water
would have buoyed—for what while longer?—

the corollas and separated petals
I'd brought to the table by fits and starts
to add to the light, but someone else
had always seemed to want

to see to that, so no sooner
than I'd floated them there I'd forgotten,
the registers of color
leaching each time to the cracked glaze

in the evaporation and ultimate press of nights
and days without replenishment.
I don't know how any of us could have thought parting
would rhyme with anything for a long time to come

except the obsessive sad riddle of sorting out
the blame for the failure of early happiness

———

and lightheartedness and all the other.
I'm not confusing the two kingdoms, the green one

wherein light is transformed into what I imagine
as always a kind of sweetness;
the other, ours,
unrooted except in an ongoing patter and patterning

I think of finally as elemental
translation in the neural fiber whose beauty
is in the embrace it tries to keep with the vanishing world.
Besides impatiens there were African violets,

a crocus or two, maybe one month an anemone.
There's a name for the system of finely cracked glaze
that carries these vague petal shapes
in fuchsia, faded purple, magenta—and it isn't memory.

It's what left
when even that has done with its constant work of forgetting.

An Ideal of Itself

Sometimes laughter moved through the field
of feeling between us
in a way that made any notion but happiness
seem impossible. Not that we were stoned

or careless—just that we had been circled
from the start by a shared medium
the craziness and goodness
of the world could be filtered through.

We could ride with the top down
and the manic outpatients
trying to stroll
as a community of believers

along the sidewalk in their prescribed happy plaids
and fresh lithium couldn't have been funnier
for all the heartache in Alabama.
Say what you want to, we didn't laugh out loud

at them or the Greek restaurant
owner's oversized painting of the Acropolis in purples
and blues with philosophers lopsided
under clouds bearing their famous names like thought—

nor give anything less than his smile in kind
when he sent wine to the table

_____

on our last night in his small town on the Chesapeake.
"For the young lovers," he said.

It's not that one way of reading
the world made up the tenor of our days and nights;
it all curves
in various arcs with the ongoing seasonal light.

Any mode of receiving the news of the moment alters
and is altered. Keats heard in the nightingale's voice
a full-throated ease transformed to plaintive anthem
within the course of a single song.

Even years later, though, when so little appeared
to be shared, there was still the middle-aged widow
from across the street, lost in time
and grief, asking on our doorstep to borrow

a birth control pill for a vacation with her new boyfriend.
And so always there's the sad thing with its tiny window
of negotiable hope. The noseless three-fingered politician
on local TV who was burned in the war:

when he jumped ex tempore
into a four-point speech with a finger for each point,
there wasn't a doubt about how to face the moment together.
Some of what Santayana says of the beautiful

———

comes to mind, a passage about its fulfilling a condition
in which there is no inward standard at odds
with the outward fact. In the way, say, light might rhyme
with an ideal of itself,

for good or ill, how Yeats cried and trembled
and rocked to and fro/Riddled with light
from the cold heaven that curved him unreasonably one day
into the blame of years past and aloneness,

its quantum his being
for the moment. I know there's a question
of what kind of witness to bear, what calls
on the past to make, what rhyming;

and I know that in sounding the memory we've made of feeling,
not everything is told in these extremes.
More and more often all I remember
is this or that landscape we passed through on our way somewhere.

———

Notes

"Easter Sunrise, the Constant Moon We Settled For"
   is for Anne Gilland and Bland Simpson,
"Time Open-Faced Yet Secret Before Us"
   for Roy Blount, Jr.,
"Where Our Voices Broke Off"
   for Tom Huey,
"Cheese"
   for William Harmon,
"Tiffany & Co." for Elizabeth Spencer,
"The Weather Wizard's Cloud Book"
   for Louis D. Rubin, Jr., and
"Cottonmouth, Angus, Redwing"
   for James Dickey.

ABOUT THE AUTHOR

JAMES SEAY was the recipient of the 1988 Award in Literature from the American Academy and Institute of Arts and Letters. His two previous books of poetry are *Let Not Your Hart* and *Water Tables*. He is also author of two limited editions of poetry, *Where Our Voices Broke Off* and *Said There Was Somebody Talking to Him Through the Air Conditioner,* and he co-wrote the film *In the Blood* with George Butler. Currently he is the director of the Creative Writing Program at the University of North Carolina at Chapel Hill.